M000202028

Extreme
Sports

by Kate Armstrong

Contents

Introduction

Imagine soaring like a bird, or reaching the very top of a mountain. Some people love the feeling of flying, jumping, and climbing. They get a thrill from falling and turning. And they enjoy challenging themselves against nature.

Some of these activities push people's minds and bodies to the limit. These activities are called **extreme sports**.

New technology can make extreme sports easier to do. Then the sports become more popular. When this happens, people try to change them to make them more challenging and exciting. They try to make them even more extreme.

Extreme sports can be tough and wild, but the aim is to take care, play safe, and have fun!

Chapter 1

Being Cool in the Snow

Snowboarding

Snowboarding is one of the newest extreme sports. It is also one of the most popular snow activities in the world.

A snowboard looks like a skateboard without wheels. It is flat on the bottom, like a ski, and slides easily down a snowy slope.

Snowboarders wear special boots clipped to the board. This helps them to control and turn the board.

boots

clips

snowboard

Extreme snowboarders don't just ride down a slope—they do tricks, spins, and turns and they ride over bumps and down chutes. Some snowboarders can do tricks in a *half-pipe*. A half-pipe looks like a giant pipe cut in half. The sides of the half-pipe are covered in snow and it faces down the slope. Snowboarders build up speed by riding from one side of the pipe to the other as they go down the slope. They fly into the air and do amazing tricks on their way down.

This snowboarder is performing tricks in a half-pipe.

? DID YOU KNOW?

Snowboarding tricks have some fun names. An **ollie** is when the snowboarder jumps into the air. A **fakie** means to ride backward. A **tailgrab** is when the snowboarder is in the air and grabs the back of the board.

Extreme Skiing

Have you ever been in a helicopter? Or have you ever skied down a really steep ski slope? Extreme skiers do both these things!

Extreme skiers fly by helicopter to mountains where people do not normally ski. These are called unmarked mountains. Skiing on these mountains can be very dangerous because the skier does not know the snow conditions and has no trails to follow.

Sometimes the peaks are covered in ice. At other times they are covered in soft powder snow. And there is always the danger of an *avalanche*.

The mountains are extremely steep, and some have vertical drops! Only very, very good skiers should try extreme skiing.

Chapter 2

Flying Like a Bird

Skydiving

Skydiving is as the word says: diving out of an airplane into the sky! Skydivers can fall for more than 40 seconds before they open their parachutes.

During a *freefall*, skydivers can fall faster or more slowly by changing their body positions. Sometimes skydivers jump in groups. They hold on to each other to make different patterns and shapes with their bodies.

An *altimeter* shows skydivers how far away they are from the ground. They read the altimeter to know when they must open their parachutes in time to float to the ground.

When skydivers are falling through the air, they can travel at about 125 miles per hour. That's much faster than cars travel on a freeway!

Skysurfing

Can people really "surf" in the sky? Skysurfers can! Skysurfing is a bit like skydiving, but there is an important difference.

Skysurfers jump out of an airplane with a parachute on, but they also have a board strapped to their feet. This board looks like a snowboard.

While skysurfers whoosh through the air, they move the board with their bodies and legs. This helps them catch the wind and do all sorts of amazing tricks. They twist and turn, and they do spins, somersaults, and even cartwheels.

Like skydivers, skysurfers also use an altimeter to tell them when to open their parachute.

Chapter 3

Wet and Wild

Surfing

Standing on a surfboard and riding toward the shore is a real thrill. Surfers must be able to balance on the board to ride a wave. They do tricks along the face or wall of the wave. They use their bodies and legs to help them move the board.

Over the years, the shape of surfboards and the material used to make them have changed a lot. Heavy wooden boards have been replaced by shorter, lighter boards made of *fiberglass*. Now it's easier for surfers to try out new moves and tricks.

One of the ultimate tricks for a surfer is tube-riding. This is when a surfer rides inside a wave, completely surrounded by water. It's like being in a water tunnel.

Surfing is extreme when surfers ride extreme waves! Surfers are towed by a jet ski to huge ocean swells. They catch waves that are massive walls of water. They soar through the ocean at an incredible speed and height.

Windsurfing

Windsurfing is a mix between surfing and sailing.

A sailboard has a mast, a sail, and a *boom*. Sailboards have a fin (or 'skeg') underneath the back of the board like a surfboard. Some sailboards have a *daggerboard* that stops them from drifting sideways.

The power of a sailboard comes from the wind. The sail catches the wind and moves the board forward. The stronger the wind, the faster the board will go.

To control the sailboard, the windsurfer stands near the middle of the board and holds the boom that is connected to the sail.

There are many types of windsurfing. Extreme windsurfers like speed, and they go speedsailing. Other windsurfers go wavejumping. They move along with the wind and race up the crest of a wave. Then they jump high into the air, doing tricks before they land.

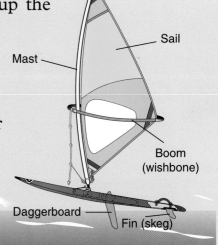

Wavejumpers use smaller, lighter boards so that they can perform tricks more easily.

? DID YOU KNOW?
The boom on a sailboard is also called a **wishbone** because of its unusual shape.

White-water Rafting

White-water rafting can be fast and dangerous. The raft zooms down the rapids of fast-running rivers, where the water has turned foamy and white from rushing over rocks.

A raft is a boat made of rubber and pumped full of air.

As many as twelve people can go in a raft. Everybody must wear special helmets and life jackets. All rafters must learn how to handle the raft before they start. They must also know what to do if they fall out of the raft while it is moving—and this sometimes happens!

All rafters must work as a team to help steer the boat. They use *single-bladed* paddles to push the raft forward, sideways or backward. Sometimes the rafters have to jump from one side of the raft to the other to balance the raft in rough water.

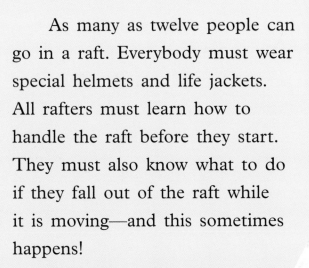

White-water Kayaking

A kayak is a covered canoe. It can hold one or two people. Kayakers sit with their legs out in front of them. They wear a skirt made of rubber around their waist. This skirt covers the hole in which they sit and stops the water from getting in the kayak. They also wear helmets and life-jackets.

Kayakers use *double-bladed* paddles to move the kayak through the water. (A double-bladed paddle has a blade at each end.) They do one stroke on one side, and then another stroke on the other. They also use the paddle to steer the kayak.

One of the most important moves in kayaking is the "eskimo roll." When kayakers tip over, they roll up out of the water while still sitting in the kayak. They use their paddles and bodies to help them ... all while they are moving!

White-water kayakers ride down white-water rivers, paddling through tight and narrow channels. They whizz around rocks, and they shoot down rapids and waterfalls.

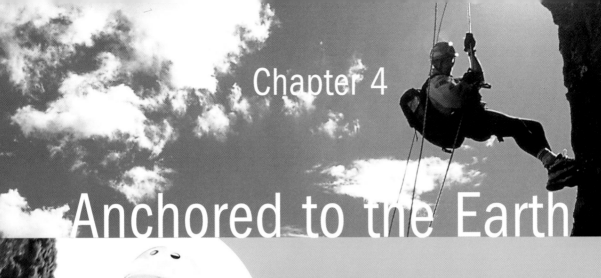

Chapter 4

Anchored to the Earth

Skateboarding

Skateboarding has been around for many years. But the way people skate is always changing.

Streetskaters ride along the street or in empty parking lots. They skate on steps, sidewalks and stair railings. They do tricks with twists and turns.

Today, streetskating is considered less extreme than it used to be. This is because skaters wear helmets and elbow and knee pads to help protect them. The boards are also much lighter than they used to be. This means skateboarders can do some of the tricks more easily.

? DID YOU KNOW?

An **ollie** is a jumping technique used by skateboarders to hop over obstacles and onto curbs. Ollies were invented in the late 1970s by Alan "Ollie" Gelfand.

Another type of skating is "vert skating." Vert skating is when skateboarders skate a ramp. The ramp is shaped like a U with really steep sides.

The skaters ride from one side of the ramp to the other. They fly up over the edge and do tricks at the top of the ramp. Snowboarders and rollerbladers also do similar tricks on ramps.

Rock Climbing

Have you ever been up high and felt as if you were on top of the world? People who climb to the top of a cliff or a mountain feel like this.

Rock climbers work their way up the side of a rock or a cliff. They grip onto rocks with their hands and feet. They must plan every move carefully, and they must decide where they will place each hand and foot as they go.

Rock climbers use a lot of equipment to protect and help them when they climb. They have ropes, *harnesses,* and helmets, and they use special gear that they attach to the cliff.

A rock climber usually climbs with a partner, called a *belayer.* While one person climbs, the belayer controls the rope. If a climber loses his or her grip and slips, the belayer pulls the rope tight. This stops the climber from falling to the ground.

Sliding down the rope is called *abseiling*. It is a quick way of getting down from the cliff top after a climb. Some people also abseil down tall buildings, without climbing them first, just for the thrill of it! (They use the stairs or the elevator to get to the top.)

DID YOU KNOW?

Rock climbers use special bits of metal called pro—short for protective gear. They jam pro into cracks in the rock as they climb. A strong metal clip is used to connect the rope to the pro. This clip is called a *carabiner*. It acts as a loop through which the rope runs.

helmet

Safety gear

ropes

pro

Climbing Step-by-Step

1 Sally and Phil are getting ready for a climb. They put on their harnesses and helmets. They prepare their ropes and pro. One end of the rope is tied to Sally's harness. The other end is tied to Phil.

2 Sally starts to climb. Phil stays on the ground. He is the belayer. He feeds the rope out for Sally as she climbs.

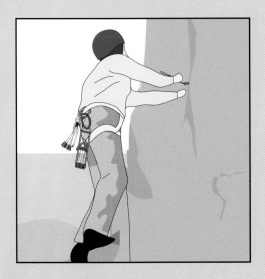

3 Sally wedges a piece of pro into a crack in the rock. She uses a carabiner to clip the rope to the pro. Phil watches and keeps her rope tight.

4 Sally repeats this until she gets to the top. Sally knows that if she slips, she will only fall twice as far as her last pro. She gets to the top safely.

5 Sally anchors herself with the rope to a tree or a rock. The other end is attached to Phil. Phil starts to climb. Sally pulls in all the slack rope between the tree and Phil. She is now the belayer.

6 Phil takes out all of Sally's pro on the way up. He gets to the top. What a sensational view!

? DID YOU KNOW?
A **bunny hop** is when a rider jumps over logs and ditches while staying on the bike.

Mountain Bike Riding

Mountain bikes are different from other bikes. They can be ridden on almost any kind of ground because they have special tires and gears.

The tires of a mountain bike are very thick and they have tough tread for good *traction*. This makes it easier to ride up and down steep mountains, on gravel roads, and through ditches. It also lets them go through water, mud, and sand.

The special gears help riders control their mountain bikes when speeding down a hill. They also make it easier to ride uphill.

People go racing on their mountain bikes in open and wooded areas. They speed up and down hills and jump over objects such as logs and ditches. They do tricks such as wheelies and bunny hops. These stunts help them get through the course as quickly as they can.

Chapter 5

Extreme Safety Tips

Extreme means radical! It means the farthest you can push yourself. People practicing an extreme sport push themselves mentally and physically. They must practice a move over and over again, and think a lot about the best way to perform the next move, stunt, or trick.

Practicing an extreme sport is exciting. But sometimes, accidents happen. You must always take care of yourself and of others.

Rules

1. Always practice the sport with a qualified person.
2. Take lessons.
3. Know the dangers.
4. Think of others.
5. Wear and use the right equipment.
6. Take care of your equipment.
7. NEVER show off!

When practicing extreme sports, the main aim is to have fun in the safest way possible.

If you follow the safety rules, you can have extreme fun with your friends!

These students are learning how to use climbing equipment.

Glossary

abseiling	to slide down a cliff, using a rope fixed to a higher point
altimeter	an instrument that tells skydivers how far they are from the ground
avalanche	a huge amount of snow that falls down a slope
belayer	the person who holds the climber's rope securely
boom	the bar that the windsurfer holds onto to help steer the sailboard
carabiner	a metal clip with a spring, through which the rope runs
daggerboard	a large fin that is slotted into the center of a sailboard
double-bladed paddle	an oar with two blades, one at each end
fiberglass	a strong, light material made by weaving strands of glass together and cementing them with resin
freefall	falling through the air before the parachute opens
half-pipe	a curved ramp that skateboarders and snowboarders can do stunts on
harnesses	straps with clips used to attach someone to something safely
single-bladed paddle	an oar with a blade on one end
traction	grip